THE GIFT OF GODPARENTS

THE GIFT OF GODPARENTS

FOR THOSE CHOSEN
WITH LOVE AND TRUST
TO BE GODPARENTS

TOM SHERIDAN

acta
PUBLICATIONS

To my own godparents and my own godchildren.
And to all godparents everywhere.

THE GIFT OF GODPARENTS
For Those Chosen with Love and Trust to be Godparents
by Tom Sheridan

Edited by Gregory F. Augustine Pierce
Cover design and artwork by Tom A. Wright
Text design and typesetting by Patricia A. Lynch

Scripture quotations are from the *New Revised Standard Version Bible*, copyright © 1989 by the Division of Christian Education of the National Council of the Churches of Christ in the USA. Used by permission. Quotations from the baptismal ceremony are taken from the *Rite of Baptism for Children* copyright © 1969 by the International Committee on English in the Liturgy, Inc.

Copyright © 1995, © 2007 by Tom Sheridan

Published by ACTA Publications, 4848 N. Clark St., Chicago, IL 60640, (800) 397-2282, www.actapublications.com.

Library of Congress Number: 94-073612
ISBN: 978-0-87946-104-1
Printed in the United States of America by Versa Press
Year: 25 24 23 22 21 20 19 18 17 16 15 14
Printing: 20 19 18 17 16 15 14 13 12 11 10 9 8

CONTENTS

A SPECIAL INVITATION
FROM THE PARENTS

We want you to become someone special in the life of our child. That is why we have asked you to be our child's godparent.

Our baby's baptism is an important moment for us and for our child. We want it to be memorable for you, too, and so we offer you this book as our gift to you.

Even if you've been a godparent for another child, our child is a unique person, full of unique gifts, the recipient of a unique touch from God. Both of you, adult and child, can be changed forever by this simple act of joining in the celebration of our child's baptism.

We're grateful that you said yes to this opportunity and to this challenge. We want you to understand what it means to be a godparent.

You will be someone for our child to look up to. With us, you will help form our child's values and morals and faith in Jesus.

We want you, with us, to help our child to dream and hope and grow. We treasure your friendship and hope our relationship will be a source of strength for us as we walk through parenthood.

We are honored that you have agreed to be a friend and guide in our child's faith and life.

Gratefully,
The Parents of Your
New Godchild

For in Christ Jesus you are all children of God through faith…
all of you are one in Christ Jesus.

Galatians 3:26-28

A WORD OF WELCOME

Since you're reading these pages, it means someone has asked you to become a godparent.

CONGRATULATIONS.

Now that the initial excitement of being chosen for this very special role may have worn off—or even if you've been a godmother or a godfather many times over—you might be wondering just what it all means. And that's why you are reading this book. It might have been a gift from the child's parents or their parish. Or it might have been something you spotted all by yourself. It doesn't matter which.

WELCOME.

As a godparent you are part of a grand and ancient tradition. Your spiritual forebears have walked this road for two millennia, caring, guiding, loving, helping—and perhaps most importantly—remembering the child with whom they have a special personal and spiritual relationship.

As a godparent you are about to be blessed with some very special rights, some awesome responsibilities and some tremendous opportunities.

You may never have thought about it in this way, but it's true: You are about to impact a young life. And there is little else quite as special, quite as awesome or as much an opportunity.

Being a godparent can be an exciting journey, much like that of holding onto the hand of a small child walking through a park. You never know exactly what's going to pop up.

The role you play in this life drama, this faith drama—that of godparent—is one that has had various understandings down through the centuries. You may even see your role somewhat differently than the parents who have chosen you do. In any case, godparents are blessed with the continuing promise of faithfulness from the God who loves us and cares for us.

So that you might have a better understanding of what might be expected of you as a godparent (or baptismal sponsor), this little book will help you reflect on the sacrament of baptism, our Christian faith, the role of a godparent, the baptismal ceremony, the relationship between a child and a godparent, and what the future might hold for you as a Christian godparent.

Good luck and God bless you, dear and important godparent.

WHO, ME, A GODPARENT?

A brief story: A mother and a father—both faithful Catholics—are interested in having their newborn infant presented for baptism. At the preparation session held by their parish, they are asked whether they have chosen godparents yet.

They look at each other, very nearly in puzzlement.

"Godparents?" they both say almost in unison. "We really don't know anyone worthy enough."

And they mean it.

Now there's a story capable of striking fear into the heart of any prospective godmother or godfather.

"Am I worthy enough? After all, it's a big job. I mean, there's responsibilities and everything, right?"

Of course there is. But "worthy" is a loaded word.

Parents have the responsibility of selecting good role models for their child, and there are rules in place to help guide that selection. Even so, it's important to remember that none of us is perfect.

If you're going to become a godparent, do you have to be perfect? No.

Are you expected to be a saint? Certainly not. In fact, you'll probably be a better godparent if you aren't.

Now about those rules.

While hard-and-fast rules for godparenting may vary from diocese to diocese, godparents are generally expected to be over the age of 16 or to have received the sacrament of confirmation. At least one godparent must be Catholic; the other, if not Catholic, must be a believing member of another Christian denomination.

Godparents do their best when they keep trying
to make the Gospel (the Good News) real.
The Good News that Jesus calls each of us to live
is neither complex nor magical.

Some parishes ask prospective Catholic godparents to present proof that they are practicing (active) in their churches. That usually means that the godparents have to get a letter from their parish stating that they are regular churchgoers.

Other parishes are more trusting of the parents. They figure that parents aren't going to lie about the rules. Or, if they do, it's only their child they are putting at risk, not the structure of the faith.

A godparent is expected to be a believing Christian because that's one of the values a godparent is supposed to pass along to the child. As a child's sponsor for the sacrament of baptism, a godparent should offer a positive example of faith. If we expect children to take a positive view of religion, it's a primary role of parents and godparents to show them the right direction.

Sometimes the most successful way that godparents can make an impression on a young person is to keep trying: Keep trying to do good, keep trying to make right decisions, keep trying to love God—even when it's not easy.

Godparents do their best when they keep trying to make the Gospel (the Good News) real. The Good News that Jesus calls each of us to live is neither complex nor magical.

It is simply...

To feed the hungry. To visit the sick. To welcome the stranger. To free the captives. To instruct the doubtful. To comfort the sorrowing. To proclaim the favor of God upon all people.

That's not an impossible task for a godparent. Nor does it take perfection. Only the promise to keep working at it.

To be a godparent is to invest in the future and to look far ahead. To look ahead, we must sometimes look behind—and that's what the next brief chapter is all about.

Baptism can be a ritual,
a social event, a faith-filled moment,
a religious milestone,
a family tradition.

WHERE DID IT ALL BEGIN?

Baptism. Christening. Initiation. You might hear any or all of those words used to describe the very special event you've agreed to be part of as a godparent. Now that you have signed on to be a baptismal sponsor, you might as well get an idea of what it's all about.

Baptism is one of the most important—and most paradoxical—sacraments of the Christian church. For all its popularity (virtually all of Christianity celebrates it), baptism is perhaps one of the least understood of the sacraments or rites of the church.

Baptism can be a ritual, a social event, a faith-filled moment, a religious milestone, a family tradition.

And it can be all of these.

Baptism is also a paradox because it is at the same time among the most personal of sacraments as well as among the most communal.

Sometimes, parents and godparents view baptism in a more individual way, as a truly personal touch from God. They see it as a narrow beam of light lancing out of heaven to illuminate the child in their arms, perhaps catching the others present in its reflected glow.

Other families are more aware of the communal nature of baptism. They recognize that beam to be a floodlight bathing them, the child, the people present for the ceremony, the parish community and indeed all believing Christians with God's life and love.

For you, the one asked to be a godparent, asked to stand up for this new life, asked to present yourself as someone special in this child's existence, what does baptism mean?

While a little history and a little theology can be helpful here, this small book of sharing doesn't pretend to cover all the history or all the theology surrounding this very important Christian act. But it can help set the stage by telling you "Everything You Always Wanted to Know about Baptism but Didn't Know Whom to Ask."

> *Through baptism men and women are incorporated into Christ. They are formed into God's people, and obtain forgiveness of all their sins. They are raised from their natural human condition to the dignity of adopted children. They become a new creation through water and the Holy Spirit. They are called, and indeed are, the children of God.*
>
> *—From Romans 8:15; Galatians 4:5;*
> *Council of Trent; 1 John 3:1*

There's a little quip that describes a newly baptized infant as "a very early Christian." There's more than a little truth in that. But among the very early Christians—the original ones who lived in Palestine, Greece and the Middle East—baptism was something which almost never included small children.

The situation was not unlike that of immigrants to the United States generations ago. Papa was generally the only member of the family to state a desire for citizenship. Mama and the kids, if there were any, went along for the ride.

In the early church, the only one who mattered was Papa. If he became a Christian, generally so did the rest of the family. By default.

Becoming a Christian in those first centuries was not exactly a simple matter, either. When the Christians were an underground society living in fear of persecution, becoming a Christian was something that was done very quietly. You didn't advertise it. A person who had heard the Good News preached by a disciple usually made discreet inquiries about joining the local Christian community. If the potential member seemed sincere, the local assembly would assign one of its number to provide the instruction. At first it was not a particularly structured process and the new member was quickly assimilated into the group—often just in time for the next persecution.

The Christian who was assigned as the teacher was someone just like you—someone who could be described as being one of the first godparents. The basic role of the godparent way back then was much the same as it is today: someone to help teach, to befriend, to guide and to love the new Christian.

Despite the persecution, the message of Christianity hit the ancient world like a thunderbolt. As scripture says, "Every day the Lord added to their number those who were being saved." (Acts 2:47)

To these new recruits, the local church would assign a sponsor—a godparent, if you will. The sponsor would instruct the prospective Christians, now called "catechumens," in the beliefs and practices of the faith.

The process was no longer a short one. It could take as long as three years for a catechumen to be baptized and accepted into the church. And a godparent walked with the prospective believer all the way. It was not easy to be a godparent back then.

Godparents, then, were the guides of faith—the most trusted, most believing, most deeply spiritual members of the community.

Scary, isn't it?

You're probably saying something like this to yourself right now: "Wow, is that what's expected of me? Am I that kind of Christian?" Don't worry, other chapters in this book explain the church's expectations for today's godparents and suggest some ways for you to be a terrific sponsor. It's not quite as demanding as it once was, thank God.

Now back to our story about how baptism—and the role of the godparent—has evolved over time to the present reality.

A few hundred years into its history, the church was prospering. Just about everybody around was a Christian. And, not unlike today, Christians were having baby Christians. Or, at least, Christians were having babies. The church, for its part, was having a debate about those babies.

The church knew what to do about adults who wanted to be Christians. It instructed them, judged them, accepted them, baptized them. But when Christians had babies, the church wasn't sure what to do with them. Should it baptize them right away or wait until they were adults and could make their own decisions?

After a time, a very influential bishop named Augustine—we know him today as St. Augustine—thought and prayed and decided that if these children were going to be raised as Christians they should have the sacramental blessing that goes with being Christian right at the beginning of their lives. So the church began baptizing children, placing upon them the seal of the promise of faith. Because they couldn't state their beliefs like adults, however, it was left up to their parents to make the baptismal promises and profession of faith for them.

At the same time, a godparent, in the name of the community of believers, also affirmed the commitment of the parents and agreed to assist in the faith formation of the child being baptized. This was the beginning of the role of godparents as we have it today.

A few hundred years went by—and then a few hundred more—and the ritual of infant baptism became accepted more and more as something that good Christian parents did. Even Christians who were Christian in name only had their children baptized. And godparents still would stand up and promise to help the little ones carry on the flame of faith. In some cases (especially among some ethnic groups) the godparents even came to be considered more important than the parents themselves in the baptismal ceremony.

The tradition of infant baptism continues today in the Catholic church. In some families, baptisms are more of a social event than a religious one, and a christening is often just another reason to have a party. Godparents are often viewed as merely honorary or ceremonial "bit players."

In recent years, however, the church has been trying to help its members—especially the parents and the godparents—recognize that baptism is a pivotal event in the faith life of both the child and the family. Therefore, the church promotes the value and desirability of choosing as godparents people who can help the parents provide the foundation of faith and values for the child.

It is important to remember that baptism is seen by the church only as an important first step in the process of initiation into the faith. Baptism is not something that magically makes a baby into a Christian but an event that helps prepare the soil for the planting of the seed. The splash of baptismal water and the words said by the priest or deacon are not magic. The church does not believe in magic. It believes in a God who invites, who challenges, who loves, who forgives—and baptism is a sign of that God's presence.

God invites, challenges, loves and forgives not only the child who is at the center of the baptismal event but also the parents and, of course, the godparents.

The role of godparent might be a momentary thing: a Sunday afternoon of water, words and whoopee at the party which follows. Or, it can mean a lifelong commitment to helping parents share their faith with and build faith within their child.

In many ways, the choice is up to the parents. And to the godparent they choose.

You are that person.

For you, the one asked to be a godparent,
asked to stand up for this new life,
asked to present yourself
as someone special in this child's existence,
what does baptism mean?

ISN'T EVERYTHING DIFFERENT NOW?

Some people might be hesitant to become godparents because so much seems to have changed in the church since the Second Vatican Council and in more recent decades. Relax. Godparents don't have to take a religious knowledge test or recite the 10 Commandments in order —although it's important that those commandments, the beatitudes, and God's great law of love serve as guides for a godparent's own life.

Here are a few ideas about what the church teaches and believes about the sacrament of baptism and the role of godparents.

First, about the sacrament of baptism itself. It is indeed a mystery, but it is not a magical ritual. It is rather a mixture of sacred signs and treasured symbols, holy words and heartfelt promises that come together to make up this most ancient Christian ceremony and most important Christian sacrament.

Baptism helps us confirm and affirm that which we already believe—that this child, this small piece of life we are presenting to the church, is welcomed by God and welcomed into God's family.

That's what a sacrament is all about—an outward sign of the love of God as expressed in the person and spirit of Jesus. Sacraments reflect that love through the reality of the world and church God gave us.

Is that love different for us than it was for those on the dusty streets of ancient Palestine? No. The essence of baptism has always been a welcome invitation by God and by God's people to share the wonders of faith in the love of God.

Baptism, one of the oldest Christian rituals, has always had that dimension. It still does. It remains an external sign of our belief in Jesus Christ and in the God who invites us to allow the divine presence into our lives.

Baptism is the first sign the church provides that God's love is open to all. It's also the first step in the ongoing process of the sacramental initiation of each believer into the Christian community. The next steps are confirmation and eucharist—although maybe not in that order.

> *Dearly beloved, these children have been reborn in baptism.*
> *They are now called children of God, for so indeed they are.*
> *In confirmation, they will receive the fullness of God's Spirit.*
> *In holy communion they will share in the banquet of Christ's*
> *sacrifice, calling God their Father in the midst of the church.*
> *—Rite of Baptism for Children*

The sacred moment—the sacrament—of baptism is neither myth nor magic, but mission.

Throughout the history of our faith, baptism has been the initial starting point of faith and action. By tradition, Jesus' first public act was his baptism in the River Jordan by John the Baptizer.

So, what has changed since then? Nothing, really, save our continually deepening understanding of the sacrament.

Baptism was never meant to be a meaningless ritual or a social act alone. From its very beginning, the ritual—and the reality—was to symbolize the joining of a new believer to a group of like believers to form a community dedicated to following the ways of Jesus Christ. Baptism was—and remains—the grand beginning.

THE BOY WITH MANY GODPARENTS

Saint Paul told the earliest Christians that different people learn about God in different ways. "The Jews look for signs, the Greeks seek wisdom," he wrote. Today we are often like the early followers whom Jesus instructed with stories taken from everyday life. We, too, are a people who learn best not by rote recitation but by story and example. So, perhaps a story is appropriate here:

Michael's journey from his birthplace outside Manila in the Philippines to his home near Chicago was far longer than the 22 hours the airliner took to traverse the distance. It took months of concern and worry, prayer and preparation, surprise and celebration. Michael, understandably, knew nothing of this at the time; he was too young. But for his soon-to-be adoptive parents, the time passed with painful slowness.

On several occasions, word would come from the orphanage that their son would be coming soon. Then, over and over, something would happen to delay the process.

It might be a piece of the paperwork that had been lost or filled out improperly. Or a national holiday that closed offices. Or an American consulate overburdened by work. Or, if truth be told, just a bit of official laziness. Whatever the reason, the weeks stretched into months and the months into seeming eternities. Holidays came and went, and Michael still did not arrive.

During it all, his parents were surrounded by a community of friends from their parish who were able to help them through the long ordeal. But it played emotional havoc with the couple. They became reluctant to share news—good or bad—because it was too painful to bear the excitement and subsequent letdown. When word came, once again, that Michael was coming, they told no one.

As the day of impending arrival drew closer, there was no canceling cable, no transpacific telephone call changing the plans. Still, they told no one. Even after the airline confirmed that Michael and his escort were indeed on the plane, they were only cautiously excited; hopes had been dashed too often.

The afternoon of the plane's scheduled arrival at the airport, the family —Mom, Dad, and their two young daughters—went to the terminal to wait the final hours. With them went the couple who was to become Michael's godparents, along with their children.

And they waited.

The plane was delayed. Mechanical troubles, someone said. But they waited and, as they waited, a most remarkable thing occurred. Other friends began arriving: couples, singles, families with children. Somehow, the word had spread that today was the day. The waiting was truly over.

Before the plane—which was appropriately dubbed Northwest Stork Flight 006—arrived, a circus atmosphere filled the terminal waiting room as more than 80 friends anxiously anticipated Michael's touchdown on the tarmac. When the plane landed and the courier bearing the child stepped into the throng, a deafening cheer went up. Adults applauded and children shouted and whistled.

Michael's baptism—not the ritual, but the reality—occurred that day as he was surrounded and welcomed by a whole community of godparents.

Michael was accepted into a body of believing Christians who had taken the time to acknowledge their commitment to him, to say, in essence: "We're glad you're here, Michael. We want you to know and remember that you are a part of us. We will teach you about the God we believe in, about how we celebrate that God's important presence in our lives. We will pray for you."

That's what godparenting is all about.

Several weeks later, Michael's new parents celebrated the actual ritual of baptism in their parish. The celebration acknowledged the reality of what had already taken place. His parents acknowledged the support of the parish community right along with that of his godparents by challenging them all to continue supporting Michael as he grew into a young man.

Their thunderous "I do" was a powerful acceptance of that challenge.

The essence of baptism remains the birthright of every child—to know the love and touch of God, the welcome of the Christian community and its promise of support.

The essence of baptism remains the birthright
of every child—to know the love and touch of God,
the welcome of the Christian community
and its promise of support.

WHAT'LL I DO AT THE CHURCH?

If you're like most godparents-to-be, the first thing you said after you said "yes" (and maybe even before), was "Omigosh—what am I gonna do at the church?"

Don't worry if you haven't asked yourself that question yet. It means you are either (a) an experienced godparent, (b) a new parent yourself who just sat through all those boring baptism classes at your parish, or (c) too confused to worry about it right this minute. But go ahead, you can ask yourself the question right now.

Actually, your question is not unlike the first question new parents ask themselves when they realize there's a baptism in their future. It's quite normal not to know what to do. After all, people don't attend baptisms every day, and when they do, they don't always pay attention to what everyone is doing.

Godparents shouldn't lose too much sleep worrying about whether the priest or deacon celebrating the ceremony is going to embarrass them in some way if they don't know exactly what's happening next. If the truth be told, most presiders haven't committed the ceremony to memory. Even they follow the book.

Baptism presiders—priests and deacons—are generally an easygoing lot. They've handled lots of crying babies, lots of nervous parents, lots of confused godparents and lots of different situations. They're usually pretty good at guiding people—especially nervous new godparents—through the ceremony.

So relax. You probably will be surprised when the presider guides you through the ceremony so easily people will swear you are an expert. And, if you don't know something, just ask.

What follows is a basic outline of what will happen.

THE CELEBRATION OF THE SACRAMENT OF BAPTISM

The baptismal ceremony has four parts:

1. The reception of the child,
2. The celebration of God's Word,
3. The celebration of the water rite,
4. The concluding rite.

Each part is integral to the whole and each has several sections. This is true especially when the baptism is celebrated as a ceremony by itself, usually on a Sunday afternoon. When the baptism is celebrated during a Mass, the initial rites may be altered slightly and may take place at the start of Mass, or the entire ceremony may be celebrated after the homily.

1. THE RECEPTION OF THE CHILD

The presider greets the congregation and may stress the importance of the family and the community of faithful into which the child is being baptized.

The role of the child's parents and godparents is explained. In general, the church understands and teaches that the parents are the primary guides and educators in the faith for their children. The godparents, other family members and the parish community should help with this task, but parents bear the main responsibility.

The parents are asked the name of their child and the reason why they are presenting their child to the church. In their own words they answer that they seek baptism, entry into God's family and the support of the Christian community for their child.

The parents, sponsors and the entire Christian community then accept responsibility for nurturing the child's faith and values.

Do you clearly understand what you have begun here today?
—Rite of Baptism for Children

This welcome into the Christian community is symbolized by marking the child's forehead with the sign of the cross. The presider will do this first and then invite the parents and godparents and perhaps all present to make the same mark.

The Christian community welcomes you with great joy. In its name I claim you for Christ our Savior by the sign of his cross. I now trace the cross on your forehead and invite your parents and godparents to do the same.
—Rite of Baptism for Children

2. THE CELEBRATION OF GOD'S WORD

One or more readings from scripture that pertain to baptism, initiation, salvation or the symbol of water will be read aloud. This may be done by the presider or, more likely if the ceremony is not part of a Mass, by a parent, godparent or other family member.

A short homily by the presider helps explain the importance of baptism as a sign of faith.

The presider then offers prayers of the faithful (petitions) for the child, the parents and godparents, the Christian community and the world. The presider is likely to invite similar petitions from the parents, godparents and other members of the congregation.

The presider prays a prayer of healing and anoints the child on the chest. The oil that is used in this anointing is known as the oil of salvation. It reminds us that blessed oil was an instrument of healing and strength in the early Christian community.

We anoint you with the oil of salvation in the name of Christ our Savior; may he strengthen you with his power, who lives and reigns for ever and ever.
—Rite of Baptism for Children

3. THE CELEBRATION OF THE WATER RITE

The presider blesses the water to be used for the baptism.

Parents, godparents, family and friends are then invited to profess their faith in Jesus Christ who, with them, is to be the lifelong guide for the child being baptized. The presider leads everyone in the renewal of their own baptismal vows.

If your faith makes you ready to accept this responsibility, re-new now the vows of your own baptism. Reject sin; profess your faith in Christ Jesus. This is the faith of the church. This is the faith in which this child is about to be baptized.
—Rite of Baptism for Children

The presider baptizes the child with water in the name of the Father, the Son and the Holy Spirit. Either the water is poured or sprinkled over the baby's forehead, or the child is immersed into a baptismal font.

A lighted candle is presented to the family, often to one of the godparents, as a reminder of the light of Christ and the fire of faith.

4. THE CONCLUDING RITE

The presider will liberally pour or apply chrism—perfumed oil which is also used in the sacraments of confirmation and ordination— to the top of the child's head as a symbol of service and mission to the people of God, a mission shared by all the baptized.

God the Father of our Lord Jesus Christ has freed you from sin, given you a new birth by water and the Holy Spirit, and welcomed you into his holy people. He now anoints you with the chrism of salvation. As Christ was anointed Priest, Prophet and King, so may you always live as a member of his body, sharing everlasting life.

—Rite of Baptism for Children

The symbolism of the white baptismal garment is explained as a sign of newness, and it is then placed on the child's breast. Some parishes present a small white bib-like garment to the child as a memento of the ceremony.

The ceremony concludes as the entire community is invited to stand and pray together the Lord's Prayer. The presider then offers a prayer and blessing over the parents, the godparents and the congregation. A sign of peace may be offered and shared by everyone who has gathered.

Most parishes recognize the importance of involving not just the parents but the godparents and the rest of the family in the celebration of baptism. Just how much you as a godparent will do may depend on local parish customs, the parents' wishes, or even cultural traditions.

The church teaches that the parents—after the child being baptized, of course—are the main focus of the baptismal ceremony. Of course, godparents are important as well, but in a different way. Mom and Dad are going to be the people the child turns to for guidance. It will likely be their morals and values and sentiments that permeate the child. All that starts with and is part of the sacrament of baptism.

The godparent's role is one of support. That support is not simply for the child, but also for the parents. Anyone who has been a parent knows how difficult parenting can be. Parents—if they are to be good, patient, loving, teaching ones—need all the support that godparents can offer. Sharing similar values, goals, hopes and dreams are important, but so is the godparent's ability to affirm the parents, sharing with them both the joy and the pain of their child's life.

Because of the central place of the parents, the church generally expects them to hold their child during the ceremony, even though this may fly in the face of some traditions. Presiders generally invite godparents to be involved in other ways during the ceremony, such as marking the child with the sign of the cross, holding the baptismal candle, and standing with the parents throughout the ceremony. (One godfather was asked to change the child's diaper right on the altar, but this probably won't happen to you.)

One of the best ways a godparent can be involved in the baptismal ceremony is by doing one of the readings from the Bible. If scripture is important to you—and your godchild's parish is agreeable—select and read a scripture passage as part of the ceremony. See pages 69-74 of this book for a list of readings suitable for the baptismal ceremony.

What is the most important thing you can do?

Be for this child and his or her parents someone special, someone who cares enough to be part of an important ritual of welcome into the faith, someone whose presence means more than presents, someone this child's—your godchild's—parents can trust, can turn to, can be honest with, can count on no matter what else is going on in the world.

That, more than all the ceremonies in the world, characterizes the faith of baptism and the sense of true godparenting.

Be for this child and his or her parents someone special, someone who cares enough to be part of an important ritual of welcome into the faith, someone whose presence means more than presents, someone this child's—your godchild's—parents can trust, can turn to, can be honest with, can count on no matter what else is going on in the world.

WILL I EVER STOP
BEING A GODPARENT?

Godparenting is forever. That somewhat frightening thought might hit you when you're on your second trip to the buffet table at the christening party, about two hours after the ceremony.

You probably knew that, didn't you? After all, even the traditional word "Christ-ening"—to bring to Christ—gives a glimmer that this isn't a one-time thing but rather stretches for years.

How can you extend the moment of this celebration into the months and years to come?

Of course you have marked this event on your heart. Now, before another moment goes by, mark it on your calendar.

You have been blessed with a tremendous opportunity and an awesome challenge. Don't be scared. The road that stretches out in front of you—in front of both you and your godchild, actually—is long and broad. It will be for both of you what you make of it. There is no pre-scribed route map, only the encouragement of others and the urging of your heart.

What, then, can you do?

You can begin by recognizing that being a godparent isn't only about religion and about religious things. Mostly, it's about faith. And there is a difference.

GOOD IDEA #1: Oh, there are the things you might expect you can do, such as send a yearly card and a gift on the anniversary of your godchild's baptism—as well as or instead of the child's birthday. That's an easy one.

GOOD IDEA #2: It is presence, not presents, which will mean the most. Nor should that presence be limited only to "churchy" events. Your godchild deserves to see you in the context of life. The opportunity of being a worthy godparent can be so broad. Offer to babysit for your godchild, take him or her to a ballgame or the park, or to work with you when he or she is older. Become a lifelong "special person" to the child.

GOOD IDEA #3: You can continue to grow in your own faith and let your godchild see that the spiritual life is a continuous, ever-expanding experience. When children watch adults make God part of their daily lives, they learn that religion and being touch with God is not out of the ordinary but is a normal, everyday part of living. Your godchild needs to see this in other adults besides his or her parents. You are a prime candidate.

Perhaps the greatest gift you can pass along to your godchild is to let him or her see that you have let God be part of who you really are. The rest of being a godparent comes easily. But remember that the values and examples you demonstrate, and not just the pious attitude you put on, are what will really each your godchild. For instance, if you cheat in business or on taxes or live a life which is clearly lacking in moral backbone, your godchild is going to see that. But if you reflect good values and good choices and good actions in your life, that will be a powerful example to your godchild that the world has a place for such things.

As the years go by and your godchild begins to grow up, your role can change, though it need not diminish.

GOOD IDEA #4: Share with your godchild as he or she celebrates the additional steps of Christian initiation: confirmation and first Eucharist. It may even be possible for you to be the child's confirmation sponsor, thus providing continuity with the baptismal experience. (Of course, that is usually the child's own call, so you either do a good job on ideas #1, 2, and 3.)

GOOD IDEA #5: Take part in your parish's adult religious education program. You may learn something that you may have an opportunity to share with you godchild.

GOOD IDEA #6: Encourage your godchild to be part of a teen retreat or faith-experience. Then offer to work as part of the team developing it or conducting it.

GOOD IDEA #7: Become active in community or parish work with poor or marginalized people. Bring your godchild along with you as your volunteer to work in a soup kitchen, food pantry, or nursing home. Perhaps you can help by building or repairing homes for poverty-level families or by caring for the environment. It will instill in your godchild a sense of responsibility for others, a cornerstone of the Christian faith. It will also help you do the same.

GOOD IDEA #8: Finally, be a part of your godchild's life by continuing to be a friend to his or her parents. Your support during troubled times—something we all have—and your joyous participation in their family celebrations will speak most powerfully to your godchild about the nature of true friendship and Christian community.

Your godchild will most likely have only two godparents—and only one godfather and one godmother. That distinction alone will make you special. It is what you do with and for the child throughout your lifetime, however, that will make you truly important.

It is what you do with and for the child
throughout your lifetime, however,
that will make you truly important.

WHAT ARE GODPARENTS
REALLY LIKE?

What are your own godparents like? Are they still alive? Have they remained in contact with you? Are they more special to you than the rest of your parents' friends and relatives? As they have gotten older, have you made any effort to single them out and be present to them as they might have done for you when you were a little child?

Stories and memories about godparents could fill many books. Here are two stories of other godparents to help you get ready for the task you are undertaking. They might give you a few good ideas that can become part of your godparenting style.

BEING PRESENT IS THE BEST PRESENT OF ALL

When Kathy was very young, her godmother, Mil, short of Mildred, was always around. Mil was her aunt, her father's older sister. Her just being present was the best present of all for Kathy.

Mil was there to lend assistance when Kathy had to buy that special present for her parents for Christmas, or their birthdays, or their wedding anniversary.

She was also the one who, each year when springtime blossomed, made a special point of taking Kathy shopping for an Easter dress.

In the early 1950s, first communions were a time of white dresses and white veils for the girls. When Kathy's second-grade class walked in procession around their suburban New Jersey church to begin that most solemn of celebrations, she carried a little bouquet of white flowers—a special gift from her aunt Mil.

Other godmothers weren't always as present as Kathy's was. Somehow Mil managed to make time to come to all those school plays and programs. And, of course, she was an honored visitor at every birthday party.

Mil was not a heroic figure. Hers were not extraordinary efforts. Her actions certainly weren't miraculous. Rather, they were the stuff of wonder—ordinary things done with extraordinary love.

Mil was Kathy's godmother, one of the most important adults in Kathy's young life. And, more than forty years later, she still is.

A NOT-QUITE-GODFATHER

Being a godfather isn't always a matter of official invitation. It's a ministry that the unwary sometimes find thrust upon them. In case like these, the title is quite unofficial, but the goals and effort are much the same.

Russ is a clown. Not the funny, "ha-ha" type of clown you might immediately think of, but a clown just the same. When he dresses in a clown's outfit, covers his face with white greasepaint, and carefully places a huge jewel "tear" on one cheek, he becomes Twinkletoes, the Dancing Clown.

For years, Russ has performed in parades, shoes, and circuses—and visited countless children in countless hospitals. The white greasepaint covers much. Twinkletoes was 87 on his last birthday. Still, he's lithe, active and touchingly, real. Until he broke his hip a few years ago, he could—and did—high-kick over his head, just as when he was a circus dancer 60 years ago.

As Twinkletoes, Russ visits regularly a hospital ward that cares for children afflicted with AIDS. He talks and smiles and tries to do what clowns have done for centuries—bring a little joy to kids.

Not long ago in the AIDS ward, Steven, a seven-year-old boy, watched Russ carefully as he went through his routine. Then the boy interrupted Russ's act with a question.

"Are you a real clown?" he asked.

"Of course I am," Twinkletoes replied. "Don't you see my make-up?"

Steven thought that over for a second, then continued: "Will you be my godfather?"

Twinkletoes hesitated not a second before he said, "Of course I will."

And with the openness of one who's lived long and well, Russ moved across the room and swept the fragile child up in his arms.

"Aren't you afraid to touch me?" Steven asked quietly, enveloped by Russ's hug.

"No," said the clown, planting kisses on both the boy's cheeks. In that moment, Russ became Steven's godfather, because he gave him a glimpse of God's love.

Steven died not long afterward. Twinkletoes stayed in touch until the end, doing godfatherly things.

What sort of things?

Caring. Loving. Talking. Holding. Showing a hurting little boy that there is still good in the world.

Was Russ a godfather to Steven, really and truly? Not in the sense that there was a baptismal ritual and a celebration and an "official" commitment. But he was. In a very real and important way.

There are many great godparent stories. There are god-parents who have raised their godson or goddaughter, who have been anchors in their lives, who have rescued them, challenged them, loved them.

If you have a special godparent story to share, send it to: Godparent Stories, ACTA Publications, 5559 W. Howard Street, Skokie, IL 60077.

WHAT ELSE DO I HAVE TO KNOW?

Here's more of "Everything You Always Wanted to Know about Baptism but Didn't Know Whom to Ask."

1. My godchild's baptism is fast approaching. But his mother seems embarrassed whenever I tell her how much I'm looking forward to holding my godson at the ceremony. I do get to do that, don't I?

Very probably not during the ceremony. The role of the godparent in the baptism ceremony has been a shifting one. The present practice now harkens back to its roots in early Christendom.

At that time—and again now—the parents are the primary focus of the ritual (other than the child, of course). The church prefers that the parents hold the child during the ceremony. This is in recognition of the spiritual bonding between parents and child that is so important, just as physical bonding is. But don't despair. You won't be overlooked. Most parishes, for example, encourage the godparents to take part in the water rite, either by touching the child during the immersion or by pouring water on the child's forehead or by helping to sprinkle the child (depending on the method used). You might also be asked to do a reading or receive and hold a lighted candle.

2. The father of my godchild has told me that the baby will be baptized by immersion. What does that mean? Is it dangerous? It sounds so, well, Protestant.

Protestant? Where do you think they got the idea? Seriously, the Roman Catholic Church has reinstituted the use of immersion for infant (and adult) baptisms. The early church did it that way almost exclusively.

Despite living in a semi-arid region where water was precious, the early Christians didn't skimp when it came to using water for baptism. They often carried water a long distance for the celebration—and they always filled a large tub and dunked the person into the water. Today, immersion is the recommended method of baptism, although sprinkling or pouring water over the forehead is still more common. Immersion is a great sign, signifying in a very real way the dying and rising that baptism is all about.

In a baptism celebrated by immersion, the presider will lower the child—yes, the naked child—into the baptismal font or pool filled with water. The child is usually immersed three times up to the shoulders as the presider pronounces the words, "I baptize you in the name of the Father, and of the Son and of the Holy Spirit."

Is immersion dangerous? Of course not. Is immersion meaning-ful? You bet it is. (By the way, be sure to get lots of pictures of the immersion. They'll be useful in embarrassing your godchild in about 14 years or so.) Besides, immersion is also great because godparents are likely to be the ones invited to change the infant into his or her baptismal ferment when it's over.

3.   I saw the priest hand the godparent a candle during one baptis-mal ceremony. If one is handed to me, what should I do with it?

A godparent is often handed the baptismal candle. Sometimes the god-parent is asked to light the candle, which is usually done from the large Easer candle which is already lit. If you are lucky enough to be given the candle, holt it aloft proudly. (This makes a great photo opportunity of yours, too—one your godchild can embarrass you with in 20 years.)

Even though the presider will say words such as: "Keep the flame of this faith alive," you can discreetly blow it out after the final blessing (and about the time the wax begins to drip onto your hands). Parents are often encouraged to bring the baptismal candles of their other children to the ceremony as a sign of their connection with their new sibling. They will be lit from you godchild's candle.

Although most parishes provide a candle for each child being baptized, you could even offer to buy or make or decorate a special baptismal candle for your godchild yourself.

4. Our godchild's parents have to go to a pre-baptismal class at their parish. Can we go, too?

What a wonderful idea. Go, learn, enjoy.

5. My good friends asked me to be the sponsor for their infant daughter. I didn't even know they were Catholic. They never go to church. If I agree to be the sponsor, does that mean I will have to take this little girl to church and see that she makes her first communion?

Not really. It is primarily the responsibility of the parents to see that their child is raised in the father. As a godparent, you are just their helper.

At the time of the child's baptism—truly a graced moment for the entire family—you might want to encourage the parents to practice their faith more regularly. As your godchild grows up, you can provide him or her with religious gifts (bible, prayerbook, religious videos, etc.) for his or her birthday or Christmas. You might even offer to take your godchild to church with you now and then—and encourage the parents to join you. In that way you can be a godparent to the whole family. Btu when all is said and done, it is the parents and not the godparents who are responsible for the faith development of the child.

6. I was so embarrassed at a recent baptism I attended. The baby howled and cried through the entire event. The whole ceremony certainly wasn't very reverent or uplifting. What if that happens at my godchild's baptism?

It could. But hold that embarrassment in check. Baptism—like any sacrament drawn from the life we all share—reflects that very human life. It must. Otherwise we will never be able to forge the link between God and humankind, between the kingdom that is here and now and the kingdom that is for all eternity. Baptism, with its splashing water, oily anointings, dripping wax, crying babies, unruly older brothers and sisters and more, can seem loud, messy and seemingly irreverent. It's not. It's real. It's life. And it can even be uplifting if you approach it with the right attitude.

The baptism ceremony should not be unnaturally sanitized. After all, water which is only sparingly dribbled isn't a good reminder of the cleansing bath recalled by this sacrament. A good soaking splash is much more like it. So what if the baby cries? Grin and bear the squalling for what it is—the rebirth of a Christian.

7. We have a toddler. It's not too late for baptism, is it?

Of course not. The church teaches that baptism should be celebrated as soon as practical. Once, that meant "hurry-up-before-something-happened" to the child. That was because of a teaching about limbo, a place where the souls of children who died before baptism went. Limbo was considered to be a place of happiness, but it wasn't heaven and the presence of God wasn't experienced.

But limbo never was a true doctrine and the church has now taken a fresh look at it. Theologians appointed by Pope Benedict XVI have concluded that the exercise of God's mercy would appear to ensure that unbaptized children would merit heaven. But that's no reason to put off baptism. And baptizing a toddler brings special opportunities. It's a wonderful opportunity for parents and children to explore the idea of baptism together, learn what it means, and discuss what happens at the ceremony.

8.   Should I give a gift to my god child on the day of his baptism?
By all means. Your presence—your gift of self—is a great present, but a bible would be a wonderful idea also. Try to make it a special bible that your godchild will be able to cherish as he or she gets older. There are a number of modern English translations available such as the *New American Bible* and *Today's English Version* (*Good News Bible*).

There are also some excellent children's versions of the bible with attractive illustrations to accompany the text. Religious videos, story books and prayer books also make nice gifts from a godparent as children grow older.

9. My dad said that when he was a godparent many years ago, he was told that it was his job to give money to the priest who performed the service. Is this still done today? What's the proper amount? And is it still the godparent's job?

There is no charge for a baptism. God's grace is freely given. In some families and ethnic groups, however, it is the custom to make an offering to the priest or deacon who performs the ceremony. Each diocese has policies about whether the priest or deacon can keep the money for his personal expenses or whether it is used by the parish. Either way, it's a nice custom. But it's up to the parents. Ask them what they wan tot do. If they want to make a donation, you can offer to do it for them if you wish.

10. What are those rules again for becoming a godparent?

The church desires that godparents be over the age of 16 and confirmed. If one of the godparents is not Catholic, he or she should be a member of another Christian denomination. For obvious reasons, persons actively involved in their faith are preferred.

There should be only one man and one woman official godparent for each child, although others may serve as a "Christian witness" to the baptism, regardless of gender. In addition, some local customs provide for more than two "unofficial" godparents, who are invited by parents to share in the faith-upbringing of their child. (In some ethnic traditions, such as Filipino, there may be as many as 25 of these "godparents.")

11. My sister and brother-in-law asked me to be a godparent, but I live in Boston and the baptism is going to take place in San Francisco. I can't afford the airfare. Does that mean I can't be the godparent?

It might be possible to have a proxy sponsor. Proxy godparents are stand-ins at the ceremony when those selected cannot be present. It is also possible that the family and friends who are present will "fill-in" for you and that your absence will be noted, without anyone actually replacing you. Proxies were considered more important when the baptismal celebration was smaller and fewer people attended. Remember, if you are not going to be able to be actively involved in your godchild's life as he or she is growing up, you should work extra hard to be present in other ways: by phone, letter, etc. Exchanging emails, instant messages, or videos of yourselves is also a wonderful idea.

12. Now that I've agreed to be a godparent, what legal obligation am I facing?

None. Being a baptismal sponsor is not a legal, but a moral and religious reality.

On the other hand, you do have responsibilities by becoming a godparent—awesome ones. There are no Baptism Police going around checking up on godparents to see if they're doing their job. Still, being chosen to help prepare a young child for the maturity of life, the maturity of values, the maturity of faith is not something to be taken lightly. If you have concerns whether this task is for you, talk to the child's parents or your won parish priest of minister.

13. When my relatives asked, I agreed right away to be a godparent for their new baby. But now that I'm reading this book I'm thinking of changing my mind. I really don't go to church very often and I'm not sure I'll be a very good sponsor.

Remember, nobody is perfect—including godparents. In a gentle way this book tries to tell you it's perfectly okay to be human, to fail often, and still to be a good godparent. You might also let this occasion be a special moment for you to evaluate your own practice of the faith and to resolve to become more attentive to the presence of God in your life. This might also be the time you take a closer look at the people, situations, or beliefs that might have alienated you from the church. You might want to talk to a priest, deacon or lay associate at your local parish. That's what they're there for. You'll be surprised how happy they'll be to hear from you.

14. The baptism's over. It was interesting and we had a great time at the party. Where do I, as a godparent, go from here?

From here, you're on your own. Well, not exactly, since your church and your faith are there to help. But you are in charge of your own "career" as a godparent. If you want a suggestion, here it is: Stay in touch with your godchild. A godparent who's never around is not going to have an impact on that young and maturing life. Be there for the parents, too. They have entrusted you with a very precious part of themselves. Treat it like that. Make your relationship special. You're no longer just a friend or relative, eve a close one, to the child or to the family. You are in a relationship that is now much deeper, more meaningful, more faithful and more reflective of the touch of a healing, saving God.

HOW CAN I GET READY?

By reading this little book you have taken a giant step toward preparing to be a successful godparent.

In the coming days you may want to find a few more quiet minutes to reflect on becoming a godparent, welcoming Christ into the life of your godchild, and drawing closer to the family of your godchild.

To make that easier, this chapter contains the text of four scripture passages that are often used at baptisms, along with a brief reflection on each reading. Slowly read the scripture passage and then the reflection. Ask yourself how each reading applies to your life. Then try to make one resolution that will impact your life as a godparent in a positive manner. You might even want to write your resolutions on page 87 of this book and look at them once a year on your godchild's birthday to see how you're doing.

GOD WILL PROVIDE

Therefore I tell you, do not worry about your life, what you will eat or what you will drink, or about your body, what you will wear. Is not life more than food, and the body more than clothing? Look at the birds of the air; they neither sow nor reap nor gather into barns, and yet your heavenly Father feeds them. Are you not of more value than they? And can any of you by worrying add a single hour to your span of life? And why do you worry about clothing? Consider the lilies of the field, how they grow; they neither toil nor spin, yet I tell you, even Solomon in all his glory was not clothed like one of these.

But if God so clothes the grass of the field, which is alive today and tomorrow is thrown into the oven, will he not much more clothe you—you of little faith? Therefore do not worry, saying, "What will we eat?" or "What will we drink?" or "What will we wear"?" For it is the Gentiles who strive for all these things; and indeed your heavenly Father knows that you need all these things. But strive first for the kingdom of God and his righteousness, and all these things will be given to you as well. So do not worry about tomorrow, for tomorrow will bring worries of it sown. today's trouble is enough for today.

—Matthew 6:25-34

It's easy to be a worrier these days. Especially so when there is a brand new life, your godchild's, to be worried about. There's something awesome in that responsibility for parents—and also for godparents. And it doesn't matter if it's the first child, the third, or the seventh. The sense of responsibility is overwhelming. It fosters worry.

After all, there are so many things that can happen; so many things that can go wrong. Illness and accidents, of course. But there also is concern about more distant things like the economy, war and peace, race relations.

What sort of world is waiting out there for this innocent child? There is violence in it, surely. But there is also a potential for loneliness, for hurt, for misunderstanding.

So much to worry about.

So much worth worrying about. No one can—or should—deny that.

Yet Jesus told his followers that they shouldn't worry. By extension, he says the same things to those of us who are still his followers. Worry isn't necessary. God will take care.

In light of all our modern problems, isn't this advice somewhat naive? After all, what did Jesus' followers have to worry about? They could pick and eat food from the fields and sleep under the stars. What did they know about harsh weather, job loss, mortgages and the like? Nor did they have to be much concerned with terrorism and weapons of mass destruction.

Jesus was a Pollyanna, right? No, not really.

If worry is the fuel of despair, trust is the engine of hope. Ultimately, God will take care, Jesus promised.

Does that mean there will be no pain? No hurt?

No, it means that worrying about all that can befall that little child will not add a moment to his or her life.

In fact, if we can believe science, such worry will have exactly the opposite impact on our lives. Worrying has become a contemporary preoccupation. But at least part of Jesus' advice was not to expend emotional energy on things which are not all that important. For the child you are helping to bring to God, to Christian community and to new life in baptism, clothes and food are not the major things he or she should worry about. What is much more important is for the child to learn to love God and others. The rest will, in a sense, take care of itself.

That's what this reality of infant baptism is all about: We give a child over to God, asking that God be part of this small life. A godparent who nurtures the sense of trust in God helps to hand that child a hopeful future.

Whatever you do,
remember that being a godparent
can be a lifelong responsibility and an eternal joy—
but only if you work at it.

> *They devoted themselves to the apostles' teaching and fellowship, to the breaking of bread and the prayers. Awe came upon everyone, because many wonders and signs were being down by the apostles. All who believed were together and ha all things in common; they would sell their possessions and goods and distribute the proceeds to all, as any had need. Day by day, they spent much time together in the temple, they broke bread at home and ate their food with glad and generous hearts, praising God and having the goodwill of all the people. And day by day the Lord added to their number those who were being saved.*
>
> *—Acts 2:42-47*

Many parents and godparents, standing there in front of the baptismal font listening to the presider talk about the community of the people of God, don't really understand. This baptism experience, they may think, is something special between this little child and God. The rest of those present—parents, godparents, friends and relatives—may seem like just so much window dressing.

They're wrong.

People may not understand how much the building of community is part of scripture. The first Christians were a group of people—a community—who believed that they had to share good times and support one another in bad. They even tried to make sure that no one had too little because someone had too much. They were a people who prayed for and with each other, watched miracles happen, and learned more each day about the God whom Jesus had revealed.

And the thing that made this community possible—the entry ticket, if you will—was baptism.

By coming together, the early Christians were assured that they would have help in time of need and promised that they would be available to help others in their need. It was a very practical demonstration of community. It is the model for our parish communities today.

It is that community of which the child is being made a part through baptism.

PUTTING OTHERS FIRST

> *Wives, be subject to your husbands, as is fitting in the Lord. Husbands, love your wives and never treat them harshly. Children, obey your parents in everything, for this is your acceptable duty in the Lord. Fathers, do no provoke your children, or they may lose heart. Slaves, obey you're earthly masters in everything, not only while being watched and in order to please them, but wholeheartedly, fearing the Lord. Whatever your task, put yourselves into it, as done for the Lord and not for your masters, since you know that from the Lord you will receive the inheritance as your reward; you serve the Lord Christ. For the wrongdoers will be paid back for whatever wrong has been done.*
>
> *—Colossians 3:18-25*

This is always a troubling passage in scripture, one which almost always causes reactions, mostly negative.

Yet it also contains truths which are important for us today—whether we are godparents, parents, extended family, friends or even children. (Though it'll likely take someone such as a wise godparent to help explain it to the children.)

Subordinate. Obey. Both words echo soundly with the same implication: submit, lose your freedom and independent action. Others read the first sentence and reject the whole passage as mean-spirited and gender-biased.

Is it?

Well, yes. At least in the sense that the people St. Paul was writing to were very much part of a male-dominated society. That was also Paul's own background—and bias. Women and children were often considered property, much as were the slaves also being written about here.

Does that mean the passage is tainted and meaningless for us, especially as part of the celebration of the sacrament of baptism?

Hardly.

Taking away the cultural trappings, Paul is giving a wonderful recipe for family interaction. In successful relationships, he says, subordination to one another is how to make love bloom. It becomes not my?life or?my marriage or my things, but ours.

Even taking Paul literally from the husband's viewpoint, is it not impossible to love a wife fully and not be subordinate to her wishes?

Children, obey your parents. Don't parents have a responsibility to instruct children in faith and values, to instill the difference between right and wrong, to mold a child to become a productive member of society? But somehow the word "obey" seems incomplete and unfortunately harsh.

And isn't St. Paul's injunction against nagging children as modern as today's teenager?

Slaves, obey your masters. This is obviously another cultural bias, since you and I would correctly say that having slaves is contrary to the love of God and neighbor. Yet Paul's advice to slaves is certainly not contrary to how we all need to conduct ourselves toward each other in today's society.

Taken at its inspired level, then, what at first seems to be a sexist, confusing, culturally incorrect bit of scripture contains the seeds of how we all should act: with love and deference, with gentleness; yes, even with obedience and simplicity. Wouldn't those be great virtues for a godparent to share with a godchild over the years?

CHILDISH OR CHILDLIKE?

> *People were bringing little children to him in order that he might touch them; and the disciples spoke sternly to them. But when Jesus saw this, he was indignant and said to them, "Let the little children come to me; do not sop them; for it is to such as these that the kingdom of God belongs. Truly I tell you, whoever does not receive the kingdom of God as a little child will never enter it." And he took them up in his arms, laid his hands on them, and blessed them.*
>
> *—Mark 10:13-16*

This is probably one of the most popular readings for baptisms. That's good. Because it touches all the right truths. But it's also unfortunate, because this story is so familiar that we may miss those same truths.
The reading is favored because it fairly gushes with nice things about children: children being welcomed, children being blessed, children being, well, children. Those are comfortable images. After all, few of us have not wished—at one time or another—to again be a child.

We view childhood as a time of freedom from responsibility, of being cared for, of having needs met, of seeing the future stretch out before us like a jeweled carpet. It's a counterpoint to the experience of adults for many people: weighty responsibilities, of no one caring for or about us, of struggling to have needs met and—probably most telling—of looking back on that stained carpet which now stretches out behind us.

Except…

Except childhood isn't really what Jesus was talking about.

First of all, Jesus' words weren't aimed at the children. They were for us, the parents and the godparents and the adults who were all once children ourselves.

And Jesus was not calling us to return to childhood—that state of being care-less, responsibility-free, always comforted. Rather his challenge is for us to be more childlike, and there is a difference.

Children have an almost limitless capacity for wonder, growth and excitement. An adult who is childlike is able to see the joy as well as the pain in life. To become like a child is to be awed once again by creation.

A childlike adult is one who can enter into the challenge offered by baptism without being dulled by preconception or cynicism or anxiety. What better way to recapture that spirit than by becoming a godparent for a really fantastic godchild—one like yours?

To become like a child
is to be awed once again by creation.

SCRIPTURE READINGS FOR BAPTISM

Matthew 3: 13-17
The baptism of Jesus by John the Baptizer.

Matthew 6: 25-34
Don't worry, God will take care.

Matthew 10: 13-15
Those who welcome you, welcome me.

Matthew 22: 35-40
The first and greatest commandment.

Matthew 28: 18-20
Baptize in the name of the Father, the Son, and the Holy Spirit.

Mark 1: 9-11
The baptism of Jesus.

Mark 3: 31-35
Whoever does the will of God is my family.

Mark 9: 23
Faith makes everything possible.

Mark 10: 13-16
Let the little children come to me.

Mark 12: 28-31
Love God above all things and love your neighbor as yourself.

Luke 2: 22-40
The presentation of Jesus in the temple.

Luke 2: 41-52
The finding of the child Jesus in the temple.

Luke 11: 9-13
Ask, and you will receive.

John 3: 1-6
Unless you be born again, you will not enter heaven.

John 4: 14
The water I give provides everlasting life.

John 4: 5-14
I give Living Water.

John 6: 44-47
No one can come to me unless the Father calls.

John 7: 37-39
If anyone thirsts, let them come to me.

John 13: 35-39
Love one another and follow me.

John 14: 23-26
Anyone who loves me will be true to my word.

John 15: 1-11
I am the vine, you are the branches; live on in my love.

Acts 2: 42-47
Marks of a Christian community.

Romans 6: 3-5
When we were baptized, we joined Jesus.

Romans 8: 16-17
How we have become real heirs of God.

Romans 8: 28-32
We have become more like God's own.

Romans 8: 38-39
Nothing can separate us from the love of God.

1 Corinthians 12: 12-13
We are baptized into one Spirit.

1 Corinthians 13: 4-7
Love is patient, kind.

Galatians 3: 26-28
All who are baptized in Christ have put on Christ.

Ephesians 1: 3-14
God has bestowed on us every special blessing in heaven.

Ephesians 4: 1-6
One Lord, one faith, one baptism.

Colossians 3: 1-4
Set your heart on higher goals.

Colossians 3: 12-17
You are God's chosen ones.

Colossians 3: 18-25
Rules for a Christian home.

I Thessalonians 4: 1-3, 7-12
God's will is that you grow in holiness.

I Peter 1: 3-5
Let us thank God for all blessings.

I Peter 1: 22-25
You have been born again.

I Peter 2: 4-5, 9-10
You are a chosen people.

I John 3: 1-2
Here is how God looks at us.

I John 4: 7-16
Let us love one another because love is of God.

PRAYERS FOR BAPTISM

A PARENT'S PRAYER FOR GODPARENTS

Lord, you have given us these faithful Christians to be
the godparents of our child.

Protect them, preserve them, help them always so that
they may be present for our child as our little one
grows from infancy through childhood and the
teenage years into adulthood.

It is a sometimes difficult world, Lord; let these godparents model for our child the love and courage
needed to follow your ways. May these godparents
help us in our duty as Christian parents, remind-
ing us by word and example what it means to be
part of the body of Christ.

Perhaps most importantly, Lord, let these godparents
become our child's friend.

Amen.

Beloved, let us love one another because love is of God; everyone who loves is begotten by God and knows God. Whoever is without love does not know God, for God is love.

1 John 4:7-8

A GODFATHER'S PRAYER

Dear God, this child is a special creation of yours,
another gift you have given the world. This world
will be changed forever by the presence of this
new life.

I come here as a Christian, aware of your presence in
the world. Help me always to reflect your good-
ness to this child. Let me give my support to the
parents of this child, assisting them in their task of
Christian parenting.

Help me to remember that, as a godfather, everything in
my life—all my actions and values—are a state-
ment to this child, with whom I am now bonded
in a special way.

It is with faith in Jesus that I stand here as this child's
godfather, sharing the promises of baptism, ready
to fulfill the trust placed in me by this child's parents and by the church.

Amen.

A GODMOTHER'S PRAYER

Dear God, this child is being welcomed into the community of your holy people this day. As a godmother, I have been given the gift of becoming
someone special in this young life.

I am present today to witness and celebrate this event,
full of joy and love and hope and expectation.
Help me always to share my sense of faith and
wonder with my godchild. Help me to remember
that this little one of yours will always look up to
me.

I pray that the sense of the beauty of life that I have
today can become part of the life of this new
Christian.

It is with faith in Jesus that I stand here as this child's
godmother, sharing the promises of baptism,
ready to fulfill the trust placed in me by this
child's parents and by the church.

Amen.

A PRAYER ON THE DAY OF BAPTISM

This is indeed the day the Lord has made.

God has made this day full of warmth and sunshine,
    whether in the sky outside or within our hearts.

This is indeed the day the Lord has made.

We welcome this day as a day of rebirth, a day of be-
    longing, a day of commitment for us all.

We celebrate this day, as we will celebrate all the days of
    this little child's life, secure in the knowledge of
    God's love.

This is indeed the day the Lord has made.

Let us rejoice in it and be glad.

Amen.

A PARENT'S PRAYER
FOR THE PEOPLE GATHERED

Creator God, you have gathered around us today a
group of people, loving family and dear friends, to
help us celebrate this day of joy and grace.

As our child grows, these are the people who will help
us teach our little one about life, about values,
about the world. From them, our child will learn
about right and wrong.

By their words and actions, our family and friends will
also instruct our child about the God in whom we
all believe.

We ask you, on this day and on all days, to be with all
those gathered here and those who are here in
spirit. Help them always to remember that you are
an important part of their lives, just as they are an
important part of the life of our newly baptized
child.

Amen.

RESOLUTIONS FOR GODPARENTS

To celebrate the baptism of my godchild,
I hereby resolve the following:

OTHER RESOURCES
FOR CATHOLIC GODPARENTS

As a godparent of a Catholic child, you might want to learn more about current Catholic beliefs or practices. Here are some other useful resources from ACTA Publications:

REMAINING CATHOLIC
Six Good Reasons for Staying in an Imperfect Church
Rev. Martin Pable, OFM Cap.

A celebration of all that is good about Catholicism, without denying or minimizing the problems the church has and the ways it has at times let us down. (128 pages, $9.95)

INVITATION TO CATHOLICISM
Beliefs + Teachings + Practices
Alice Camille

A clear, concise overview of Catholic beliefs and teachings. Includes discussion questions and prayer activities. (240 pages, $9.95)

THE CONFIRMED CATHOLIC'S COMPANION
A Guide to Abundant Living
Sister Kathleen Glavich

A "how to" manual for newly-confirmed Catholics to live out their faith with deep commitment and discover spiritual practices to adopt as their own. (160 pages, $10.95)

Available from bookstores or by calling 800-397-2282.